Stirring Muse
To
Amuse
By
Poets World-Wide

A Passionately Fair Publisher
Manuscript formatting, cover designing,
Interior artwork designed
By
Pat Simpson
www.apfpublisher.com

ISBN:978-1-387-97535-8

Foreword

This wonderful anthology book
features world-wide poets
that has been inspiringly moved
with the inspiration and intention
of creating poems that will be
enjoyed by all readers
Especially children whom
they hope will learn through
the joy of pleasurably reading
words about “Love”
"life" and "Living!"
Proving that love in life
That love is needed by all
So we can smile in life
As we grow

Contents

Contents

Contents

Acknowledgements

Thanks I give to all the contributing poets

that have so lovingly been inspired

to share their words in order to create

this very special book designed to

give hope and bring a smile

To young children and

all who reads

this book

Magickal Ball

Fairies in lovely ball gowns of gossamer

Hear their plea as they dance in their gowns so sheer

Music sets free the magick dance to all here

Even the Banshee can dance that none do fear

Beings of day and night gather in woods deep

They can play and dance while mortals are asleep

Invitingly they stay as stars of night sweep

They go away as the new day begins to seep

Dena M. Ferrari

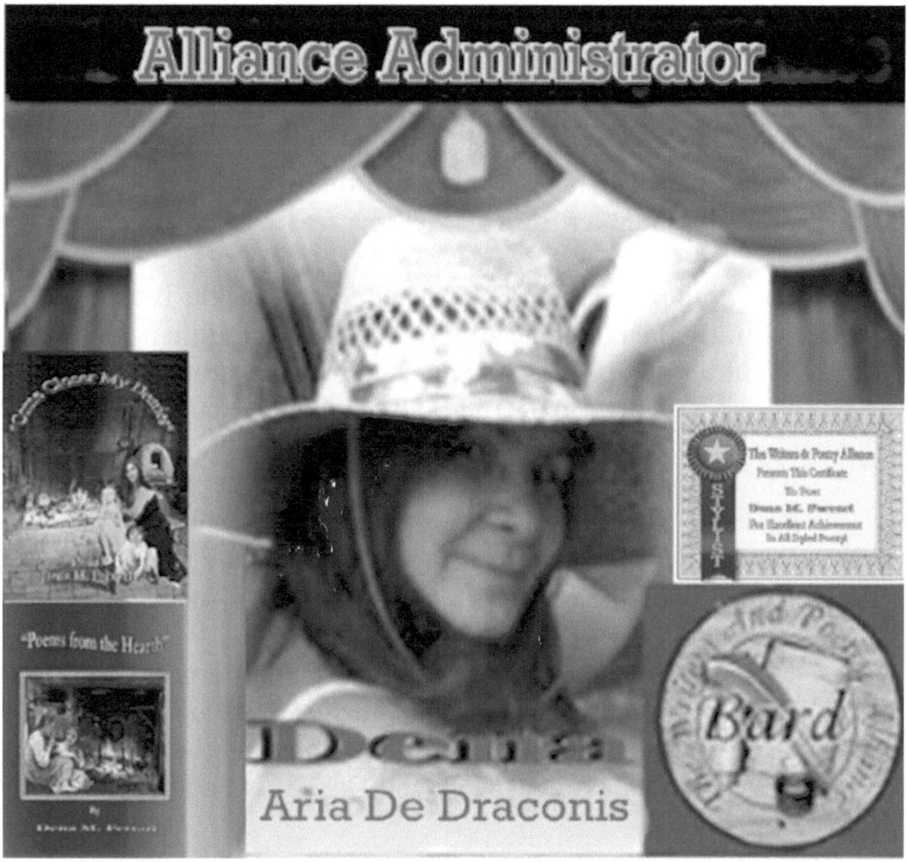

Alliance Administrator

"Poems from the Hearth"

Dena

Aria De Draconis

Bard

http://apfpublisher.com/Ferrari.html

Tiny Tickle Toes and Grouchy Grumble Belly

or

Never Judge a Book by its Cover

Down and up the lane a silly strange little man is doing a jig
Dancing wiggling lithely while waving a leafy twig sprig
Little Tiny Tickle Toes travels from town to town
Creating silly laughter from all wearing frosty frigid frowns

Merrily giggling children love seeing Tiny Tickle Toes
Delightfully the butterflies flutter chuckle each little nose
Children wave sprigs and jig as they dance around
They love Tiny Tickle Toes and the giggles abound

Down and up the lane everyone wears a silly grin
Parading with Tiny Tickle Toes and all the children
What a silly dilly sight the growing parade they make
Joined in by their critters and even a wiggly snake

More children soon join in banging on their drums
Other join with piccolos zills and kazoos that they hum
Clothes they wore all colors and ribbons all aflutter
Everyone from the village Mom and Dad sister and brother

Happily dancing playing the music as the parade jigged
All the farm animals joined in even the village prize pig
What a ruckus everything and everyone made
What a wonderful sight this village parade

Down and up the lane the parade did go towards the end of town
"Don't go that way!", the children said with a frown
"There is an old rickety rackety house that is ready to fall
Belongs to an old guy no one can understand at all"

Never worry about that said Tiny Tickle Toe
He already knew that and he wanted the parade to go
There was something to do before he was through
He knew a secret of why Grouchy Grumble Belly was so blue

Grouchy Grumble Belly always wears a scowl
He likes all things that others see as foul
Smelly and Stinky are his malodorous pets
Once you meet his reeking skunks you won't soon forget

Grouchy Grumble Belly lives so far from the fray
Griping and grumbling hoping everyone stays away
"Ack!", says he as he hears an awful ruckus on the lane
Then he spies Tiny Tickle Toes and knows his mother is to blame

"I'll show her and him", says he as he looks down at Smelly and Stinky
"These polecats will show this parade with their coats dark and inky"
Grouchy Grumble Belly was nervous as the parade drew close
He sat and thought "They won't be so happy when they smell gross"

Here came the animals all creepy crawling fluttering flying squawking
Mixed in the crowd all waving twig sprigs noise makers while walking
Now here at the gate is where this yarn of a tail of a tale gets interesting
The parade stopped suddenly as Grouchy Grumble Belly began to.....sing

Tiny Tickle Toes and Grouchy Grumble Belly were brothers it was said
One was born giggly tickly while the other was grouchy and full of dread
One had an ear to ear grinning smile that was full of wit and charm
The other wished to be left alone causing nobody any harm

Here sang the operatic song of the man they never did understand
Never ever had they heard a voice so wonderful and grand
His notes hit high higher and low deep deeper pitches with so much ease
He finally finished as he said," Now shoo go away if you would please"

Grouchy Belly's song touched each one so dearly they cried for more
Even Smelly and Stinky stomping their front legs for more more encore
Everyone learned that day to never judge a book by its cover
Nor underestimate the wisdom of the love of a beloved mother

Writer of the Knight

Mere words can't describe what darkling ink and paper hold.
Only the finished challenge relinquishes its final tales.
Long after evening slips in with her sparkled dark cloak,
The glow of candle light illuminates a bard's weathered face.
A writer of the night pens another immortal page.

In the space between midnight and the new dawn
Tumbling shadows frost the forest as it glistens;
Giving hues of shadowed purple and shaded black.
Using sight he has yet to see; his heroic reaches of destiny,
A rider of the night haunts the moonlit horizon.

To capture the moment of interest, journeys begin on pages white
Long into the darkened evening sky as bright orb of the
Moon, drips its pearly rays upon a sleeping world.
Asleep is not the bard who is illuminated by candlelight.
A writer of the knight dips into darkling ink, the quill.

Many a bardic tale have quill'd deeds of heroes who
Roamed history past, sparking imagination with fights and fame.
Glory and wonder grows wide with each telling of the tale,
While seated beside hearths, campfires and in homes and inns.
Enraptured, all listen to a bardic writer of the knighted rider of the night.

©Dena M. Ferrari

They DO Exist

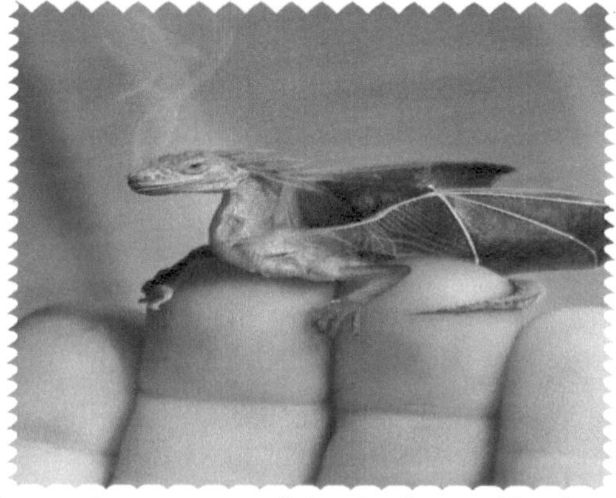

Mountain stream of deafening solitude
Kiss daylight's colorful bouquet of dawn
Diaphanous nymphs a satyr pursued
Pointing dryads laugh at the nymphs and faun.
Fields of shamrock a leprechaun does hide
While gnomes and elves forest the growing day
Faeries sit demure on beetles they ride
Dragons and flying reindeer in skies play.
Glorious Phoenix and Pegasus sings.
Titans and giants do a splendid dance.
Passions of the day bend the moon light rings,
Mermaids bedeck gems as seahorses prance

All of these things I now truly believe
A good man DOES exist; love is achieved!

©Dena M. Ferrari

The Lighthouse

Waves crashing all around
Darkness upon the sea
Just a tiny glimmer of light
From a distance can be seen

On the sea you'll find
What you're looking for
A beacon to guide you home
The Lighthouse next to shore

The sky begins to darken
As day gives way to night
The ocean beneath turns black
But above there's always light

Without ever knowing
The Lighthouse brings hope
To every boat and every ship
It tells them they are home

No matter what the weather
The Lighthouse stands tall
Through wind and rain and storm
The Lighthouse stands for all

Nicholas John Biela

My name is Nicholas John Biela and I manage a dental clinic specialising in treating patients with special needs and complex medical conditions. I've lived in Birmingham my whole life and I'm a proud "Brummie"

In my spare time I enjoy writing short stories and poems that I hope entertain and put a smile on the face of all who reads.

http://apfpublisher.com/Nick.html

The Bird Who Couldn't Fly

I was the first of my siblings to hatch
I should have been the first to fly
But mother said my time will come
Mine is not to question why

There is a secret in this nest
One which others choose to ignore
To them I am a failure
For I am a bird which cannot soar

The forest took care of all our needs
There were berries and worms and even a stream
I had outgrown the nest and wanted to leave
To fly high in the sky was really my dream

My life would soon change
One day in spring
When out grew some feathers
Right there on my wing!

I knew right then what this meant
To leave this here nest
To believe in myself
And pass this new test

My body faced downward
As I fell to the floor
But out spread my wings
And upwards I soared!

I twisted and turned
Flew up to the sky
For now I was no longer
The bird who could not fly

The Farm

There is much that I cannot do
I can't catch, I can't throw, I can't dig
But you should see how much I can eat
For I am a very hungry pig

I will wake you up at sunrise
With all my clucking and clicking
Laying eggs is hard work
For I am a very busy chicken

I have a huge stable all to myself
I wear shoes and kick with force!
I jump, eat hay and run around all day
For I am a very happy horse

I sit in a field with all my friends
All I want to do is eat grass right now
But soon I will be making milk
For I am a very useful cow

I have wool that is very thick
In spring my lambs love to leap
We have a dog to herd us around
For I am a very active sheep

There is more to see and do
Set a date, a reminder, an alarm
And visit these amazing animals
For they can all be found on a farm

The Heart of the Sea

Listen closely to me, my dear
For this is the tale
Of a beautiful monster
Known by legend as the white whale

His name is never said
Out aloud in public
But to myself and you
He is known as Moby Dick

He is greater than any creation
Older than time and all things
His skin whiter than pure colour
Death and destruction with him he brings
Boats and ships lay waste
Everywhere he goes
But where exactly he resides
No living person knows

He is who I describe him to be
He's the protector of the sea
Stopping all those who wish it harm
Heed this warning I tell thee

You must be wary if you hunt him
For there is nothing bigger than he
Venture not where he'll be found
In the heart of the sea

Mulligan

Well, here I am sitting on the golf course
Watching the fireworks display overhead
Yes, I know I'm not as big as a horse
But at least one golfer I have misled

“Kerplunk" came the ball, bouncing off my shell
Casting it deep in the adjoining woods
That’s when I heard someone yell, “Mulligan”
They ran toward the golfer like a band of hoods

I was wondering how they knew my name
As they all dashed toward the errant golf ball
And then banished the golfer from their game
Without asking if my shell had been mauled

There’s much food to be found on the golf course
So I still traverse many a fairway
But it never ceases to surprise me
How my name’s called when e’er balls go astray

Luckily my shell is hard as granite
Golf ball injuries I never sustain
So my Mulligan family moved here
Friendly golfers already know our name

Carolyn Devonshire

Guessing Games

From the moment we met, he played a game
Started out telling me to guess his name
And when I asked, “Don?”
He responded, “Right on!”
This lucky guess led to more of the same

“What do you think I do for a living?”
I hesitated, had some misgivings
“Steer the space shuttle?”
Got no rebuttal
So on this roll, I felt I was winning

“Bet you a kiss you don’t know where I live”
My mind was draining faster than a sieve
“A beachfront villa?”
(The truth would kill ya)
So many guessing games I now relive

After dating three months, his wife found out
Burst into our love nest, called him a lout
Eight kids behind her
All hungry they were
Don Juan he was, but surely no space scout

If you meet a man and he asks you to guess
Take it from me and avoid this distress
He may be akin
To Rumpelstiltskin
The anger later is hard to suppress

Now I've learned to turn the tables on men
Asking them to "guess" again and again
My private life hid
Won't remove the lid
And I've convinced some that MY name's John Glenn

Mimes at My Funeral

When my time is done and I am finally laid to rest
I don’t want to be recalled as one who lived life depressed

So as I wrote my will, I chose to leave an instruction
That laughing gas be inhaled by all those at the function

No mournful eulogies will a pastor have to invent
For my funeral will be held under a circus tent

When dozens of clowns emerge from the tiny Volkswagen
Reams of my silly limericks Bozo will be dragin’

And as they’re read aloud, family and friends who knew me best
Will say, “She had a sense of humor, this we can attest.”

Mimes will mimic me trying to write the world’s best novel
As my corpse hangs from the trapeze, surely they will marvel

Laughter will ensue as they shoot me from the cannon
Flying high in my demise across the great Grand Canyon

All the children will smile and there’ll be no tears allowed
So no one will ever remember me as a “dark cloud”

There are people who seem to take life way too seriously
When I meet my Maker, don’t view this as a tragedy

Dad called me his “happy girl,” so let me go out that way
I want to leave them laughing as I reach my judgment day

The Man Is Moonlighting

Once a month Earth's moon takes another gig
Moonlighting in a far-off galaxy
The lunar eclipse only veils the truth
The man in the moon is an absentee

Decades peering down, he needs some relief
He's seen famine, wars and catastrophes
His face now pocked by craters of despair
His other world? Fewer calamities!

He's often afraid to show his full face
So he waxes and wanes in synchrony
Slivers sometimes, half globes make their debuts
Full orb appears with lovers' harmony

Contrary to most popular beliefs
Werewolves do not gain power from his light
The man in the moon beams with a full grin
When we follow a path righteous and bright

This is the reason we see harvest moons
At times when we reap the best seeds we've sewn
The man who watches us is happy then
Bright orange smile -- appreciation shown

Night of the Headless Horseman

One Halloween night when I was five,
rain pelted city streets; we stayed inside.

Dad lit the Jack-o-lantern candle,
told us the tale of a famous vandal.

One "Headless Horseman" in Sleepy Hollow,
'twas Ichabod Crane he chose to follow.

Crane ran breathlessly, was terrorized,
(At this point my father's eyes looked wild).

Thundering behind him through the forest,
the hooves of a horse and a rider headless.

Carrying a sword to strike Ichabod.
(Dad grabbed a spatula, swung it like a rod).

Not just we children but our mother too,
gasped at the thought of Ichabod pursued.

High winds cut off our electrical power
as in our kitchen three children cowered.

Orange light from the pumpkin's evil eyes
showed Dad seemed to have dematerialized.

The youngest, I felt something run through my hair,
I screamed aloud in horror and despair.

The lit pumpkin fell from table to floor,
darkness as I ran through the kitchen door.

Leaping into bed, pulling up the sheets,
Dad snuck into my room, whispered, “Trick or treat.”

So if you think I am a drama queen,
please realize that it’s all in my genes

One Euro

On the roadside, only badly hidden
an Euro laid there from this morning

It felt so lonely and alone
and thought about the time with others

it still had its value
but today the world seems wrong

Nobody will stoop for me,
so it thought of its own free will

An old man came by,
the Euro did not seem to matter

A young couple holding hands
had not recognized the Euro

A little girl who came alone,
bent down to pocket it

Now the Euro was very happy
not being lonely anymore

Gert W. Knop

A.P.F.Publisher

Presents

Gert W. Knop

Winter Has Passed

Winter has passed with silent grip,
and nature rise again,
from dormant calm.
Crystal clear skies,
again so bright,
let us forget all winter's harm

And birds again raise up their voice.
First flowers show,
from former silent fields.
Throughout the forest' one can see
so fresh and green,
young shoots now grow
in perfect harmony

© Gert W. Knop

Blossom

Sway, sway
blossom in the wind,
send your colorful umbels
back and forth fast.
That the day will bloom in spendour,
with a joyous dancing
mind.
To you to bridge,
deep bending forth,
your scent,
your colour
brightens the dullest day,
enriches us
and let us smile

Burnt Roux

When sometimes cooked,
which was not often
you must know,
my heart throbbed,
glimpsing the roux.
I could do without it

When hungry I sat at the table
and looked happily at the food,
and like a dog my stomach growled.
But then mother forgot the time
and I already tugged at the tablecloth,
there was a big doldrums in the kitchen.

Her burnt roux,
I have to say
ousted my hunger quickly.
But do I want to complain for that?
From the kitchen smoke and smell,
soon robbed my mind,
I always knew precisely
only too literally
she took it here

The Smart Goose

You stupid goose, he shouts with rage,
not being clear to call it stupid.
And without answer he remains.
If only he had geese next to the house,
no thief could come at nightly hour,
the smart goose gave alarm
to drive away the baddest villains
and never call it stupid more

© Gert W. Knop

The Doodler

Little Winkie Doodle
Has a Poodle
The Poodle was little Winkie
Known as doodler
So, he named his Poodle
Doodle the Poodle
His brother said
Winkie Doodle
You are off
Your noodle
Mom won't let you
Have that Poodle
Winkie just started
To doodle
Because his Mom
Gave him the Poodle
That he called Doodle

Michael L Schuh

"Gone but never Forgotten"

http://apfpublisher.com/Schuh.html

Cleaver The Beaver

There was a little Beaver his name was Cleaver
Little Clearer the Beaver wanted to build a dam
He said to himself, I can do it, I know I can
Building dams is what all Beavers know how to do
But Little Cleaver found out it was impossible to do.
In the first place his teeth were not sharp enough
He'd chew and chew but no branch could he'd chew through
In the water his big tail was too big for him
Though he tried and tried but could not swim
He sat down on the rivers edge
And te God he made a pledge
If he could be big and strong
He would do no Beaver wrong
Then he started to weep
Before long he was fast asleep.
No one knows just how long he was asleep.
He woke up and beside him was logs piled up deep
On the other side was a Beaver by the name of Betty
She said “Lets build a dam together when you're read”
When the dam was ready for them to live in
He helped other Beavers over and over again
He was very kind to one and all
He was now a strong Beaver but really small
He could swim faster them any of the others
All the Beaver everywhere he'd call sisters and brothers
He now had the sharpest teeth in the river
If any Beaver needed help he was the first to deliver

I Am The Man

They call me the Man
I am doing the best I can.
Singing the Blues is what I do.
Come by my corner, I'll sing for you.
I don't get much dough in my bowl
But I have the Blues in my soul
My pipes are mellow, they say I'm good.
I would sing forever if only I could.
I play in the streets not in a bar
Some put a little money in my jar
One thing for sure I am a corner star
As of yet my music hasn't taken me far.
But you know? That's O K with me
I'll play away and do it free.
I live a simple live with holes in my shoes.
But I do not need shoes to play the Blues.
I stand on the corner of 4th & Find
Some say my music blows a persons mind.
I have had this same shirt for four year now.
But brother, I have always had my smile.
I live alone in a rundown boarding house.
Can't play in there, I must be quite as a mouse.
Yes, they call me the Man and a music man I am.
I just happy getting by doing the best I can.

The Mouse and The Cat

I am a mouse who lives in a house
By-the-way my name is Ray Mouse
In the house also lives a big cat
The cats name is Pete Mouser Rat

That is a long name for any cat
In this story I'll call him Rat the Cat
Rat the cat liked this old red hat
Me I liked lying on a brown mat

One day I was caught by Rat the Cat
I was looking in wonder at his red hat

He was going to eat me
but I asked him not to
He said he could not eat me
because he could not chew

I said Mr. Rat Cat why can't you chew
Maybe there is a way I can help you

Rat the Cat said
that would be great I can't wait
I am tired of just milk
and it has been so long since I ate

Ray the Mouse said give me time
to come up with a plan
Then someone was coming
and away Ray ran

The two got together later in the day when Ray had a plan
Ray said “Rat open you mouth and in it I’ll stand”

Rat opened wide
and Ray the Mouse went inside
Ray yelled out in fun,
this is a good place to hide

He saw the problem right away;
a fish bone was stuck in the top gum
Ray grabbed it in his little mouth between his teeth
and started to run

The bone was out and Rat the Cat had no more pain
Friends to this day those two still remain

Seasons Beauty

Summer days
Are dwindling down
Golden glow
Seasons beauty
Colorful
Rust brown and red
Leaves will soon desert the trees

Bare branches
Reach for the sun
Crimson gold
Blazing meadows
Autumn days
Soft gentle rain
Rainbow in heaven above

Erich J. Goller

"Gone but never Forgotten"

http://apfpublisher.com/Erich.html

Heavenly Play

Each day is a new beginning
Chance for winning
Earning His grace
His love embrace

Every golden sunshine morn
Love is reborn
A cherished dream
With peace supreme

The beauty does overflow
At sunset's glow
Heavenly play
Show me the way

© Erich J. Goller

Shy Like a Clam

There
was this
young man, who
was shy like a
clam

He's
never
been with a
girl, they make him
whirl

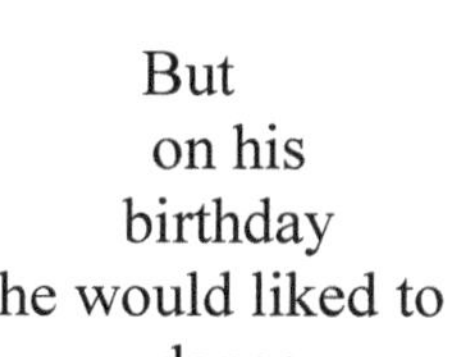

But
on his
birthday
he would liked to
dance

He
went to
a party
where he met a
girl

He
had a few
drinks that gave
him courage to
dance

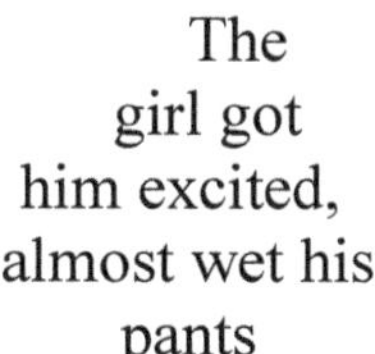

The
girl got
him excited,
almost wet his
pants

Yuletide

Christmas comes to the hearts again
There's joy around that night
And love
Born on that day in Bethlehem
The stars were shining bright
Above

Family happiness and cheers
The heavens filled with light
All still
Christmas joy that's sprinkled with tears
The church bell rang all night
Goodwill

© Erich J. Goller

The Blue Bird Knows

Where the lilac grows
The blue bird knows
By a brook
The Lord
Made
Made
The Lord
By a brook
The blue bird knows
Where the lilac grows

Fragrant springtime breeze
Full blooming trees
Heavenly
Sunlit
Might
Might
Sunlit
Heavenly
Full blooming trees
Fragrant springtime breeze

The Reindeer's Flight

For weeks they'd been restless, pacing the ground,
a rush of adrenaline, hearts started to pound,
now finally here, that magical day,
when reindeer fly, with Santa's sleigh.

Both Vixen and Comet were eager to go,
cross at Blitzen and Cupid for being slow,
Donner, Dancer and Prancer, Rudolph too,
were eventually hitched, so much to do.

Rudolph's nose shone, a beacon of light,
showing the way, through the dark night,
squeezing down chimneys, through windows and doors,
Santa left gifts, no time to pause.

Yet enjoying mince pies, a beverage or two,
he collected the carrots, fed the reindeer a few,
the rest were for later, they needed to race,
Santa urged them to hurry, step up their pace.

Just before dawn, the reindeer flew high,
Rudolph's nose dimmed, sun lit the sky,
finally home, reindeer lay in the hay,
munching their carrots, happy Christmas day.

Julie Bartlett

Naughty Gnomes

Seen in the garden, a cheerful sight,
a collection of gnomes, dressed garishly bright.

Rosy, red faces, with wide, cheeky smiles,
and quirky expressions, that amuse and beguile.

Some carry fishing rods, others have spades,
all clad in boots of various shades.

Late in the evening, as darkness falls,
they all come alive, an adventure calls.

Gaily dashing around, without worry or care,
tipping out pots, spreading soil everywhere.

At the sunrise they stop, standing still,
once again statues, a much practised drill.

Then comes the gardener, confused and perplexed,
at his garden in chaos, understandably vexed.

He stares at the gnomes, positions askew,
wearing odd boots, unmatched red and blue.

Shaking his head, he tidies the pots,
noticed green beans, tied up in knots.

Some kind of mischief, happened last night,
everything muddled, out of place, nothing right.

Gathers the gnomes, throws into the bin,
cleaning the mess, neat as a pin.

Retrieves the gnomes, their faces all glum,
back in their places, unable to run.

Later that night, no one at play,
gnomes learned a lesson, crime doesn't pay.

Bobby the Goat

Bobby was greedy, ate all the food,
lines full of washing, pieces of wood,
until one day, munching on grass,
he gulped and swallowed, couldn't pass.

Very strange for a goat,
something stuck in his throat,
it tickled and wriggled,
as he swallowed it jiggled.

Bobby spat it out,
and heard a shout,
a little, green frog,
fell on a log,
glaring at Bobby, protruding eyes,
indignant stare, outraged cries.
"You didn't look, nor did you care,
that something else was sitting there."

Bobby was sorry, he'd made a mistake,
wandered off, to drink in the lake,
the water was funny,
very slimy, not runny,
an angry frog, hopped and jumped,
sprang at Bobby, kicked and thumped.

"You didn't look, nor did you care,
that something else was swimming there."
Bobby stared, whatever next,
jumping frog, extremely vexed,
his beard tickled, lurking there,
a tiny tadpole, clinging on hair,

Bobby bent down, it swam away,
thinking I'm having an awful day.

Brilliant sunshine was warming his beard,
the young goat stirred, feeling weird,
a little, green frog, hopped into the lake,
a procession of tadpoles, swam in it's wake.

Bobby yawned and stretched, looking around,
the swimming frogs, made a splashing sound,
just a dream, ate too much food,
from now on I'd better be good,
no more gluttony, just eat enough,
grow like dad, "Billy Goat Gruff."

Taming The Witch

An evil cackle, blood curdling screech,
mixing her poisons from foxglove and leech.
Beetles and rodents, added in too,
creating a potion, and obnoxious brew.

Cauldron is bubbling, odour smells foul,
stirring the mixture, with gleeful howl.
Finally done, she leaves it to cool,
riding her broomstick, such a fool.

Once she's gone, the fairies arrive,
followed by bees, forsaking their hive.
Fairies mix potions, fragrant from flowers,
sweet, smelling herbs, glistening from showers.

Thick sticky honey, enriches the mixture,
no longer toxic, a tasty elixir.
On her return, vanished from sight,
visitors gone, they've all taken flight.

The witch is suspicious, wary, alert,
no pungent aroma, pristine, lacking dirt.
Checking the cauldron, fumes are inhaled,
breathes in the scent, wickedness slayed.

Fairies and bees, created a spell,
banishing evil, now all is well.

Trader Joe

Once was a man named trader joe
furs boots hats jackets cargo's tow
old mule number twelve
bolted like bat out of hell
canyons echoes oh hell noooooooo

Dakota's Calamity Jane

Once came a woman who we called jane
Dakota's calamity all same
saloon number seven
hustler went to heaven
dealing decks bottom oh what a shame

Katherine Stella

http://apfpublisher.com/Authors.html

Skinny Mini

Once was a girl name skinny mini
ate like horse ,no weight gained of any
pinch between cheek and gum
spittunia here it comes
ruined nights game of rum jinny

Sue Who

Once knew a gal named sue who
married a famous lawyer I knew
three hundred and fifty bucks
goes figures just my luck
want to choke both until they turn blue

Billy Jack

Once knew a man named billy jack
mentoring children that's a fact
hands and fist of speed
this only when we need
sure wish , could only come back

Oktoberfest

beyond horizon
eagle escalating heights
reaching milestones

foreign soil
honoring our heroes
a big salute

the big easy
lights camera action
mardi gras

stone cold mountain
alot of nice folk there
georgia on my mind

sailing excursion
just me and my dog
hot diggity

mirror images
reflects still lake
Oktoberfest

© Katherine Stella

The Editor Lady

An editor lady I know
has started to read on the snow,
she said, " I won't freeze -
I'm fast on my skis;
and writers just go with the *floe*..."

© Jack Horne

Aliens on Mars

When aliens landed on Mars,
they searched for the cafes and bars;
their leader professed,
'Uranus is best -
this planet is boring like ours.'

© Jack Horne

Jack Horne

The Old Baker

There is an old baker in Crete,
Who learnt how to cook with his feet,
As he kneads at the dough,
All his customers know
His bread will be cheesy, not sweet...

The Rushing Witch

There was an old witch on a brush,
Who flew to the moon in a rush,
But she fell from the sky
In the blink of an eye,
"I'm learning," she said, with a blush.

The Flying Witch

A witch who was learning to fly
was thrilled as she soared in the sky;
when hitting a rock,
she shouted in shock,
'Give asteroid-surfing a try!'

Dumb the Guitarist

There was a guitarist called Dumb,
Who mimed with his finger and thumb,
And he thought he had flair
As he played on the air,
But plucked when he needed to strum.

© Jack Horne

The Scared Ghost

A ghost who was scared of the dark
decided to haunt in a park;
the kids were so loud,
he hid in his shroud,
complaining, 'This garment's so stark.'

© Jack Horne

The Knight's Tassel

There was an old knight in a castle,
His helmet was topped with a tassel,
And he looked very tall
As he stood on the wall,
But moved to a house for less hassle.

© Jack Horne

Bollards

Standing like soldiers
On central reservations
Of all major roads
Throughout the nation
Like wizards hats
They take their place
To become a blight
On the human race
As traffic huddles
In single file
Forming queues
That stretch for miles
Cars ease forward
At snails' pace
As drivers edge toward
Workers in place
Relaying tarmac
Cutting grass edges
Replacing lights
Or just causing chaos
As they practice at nights
Whatever the reason
There is no escaping bollards
Whatever the season

© George L. Ellison

George L. Ellison

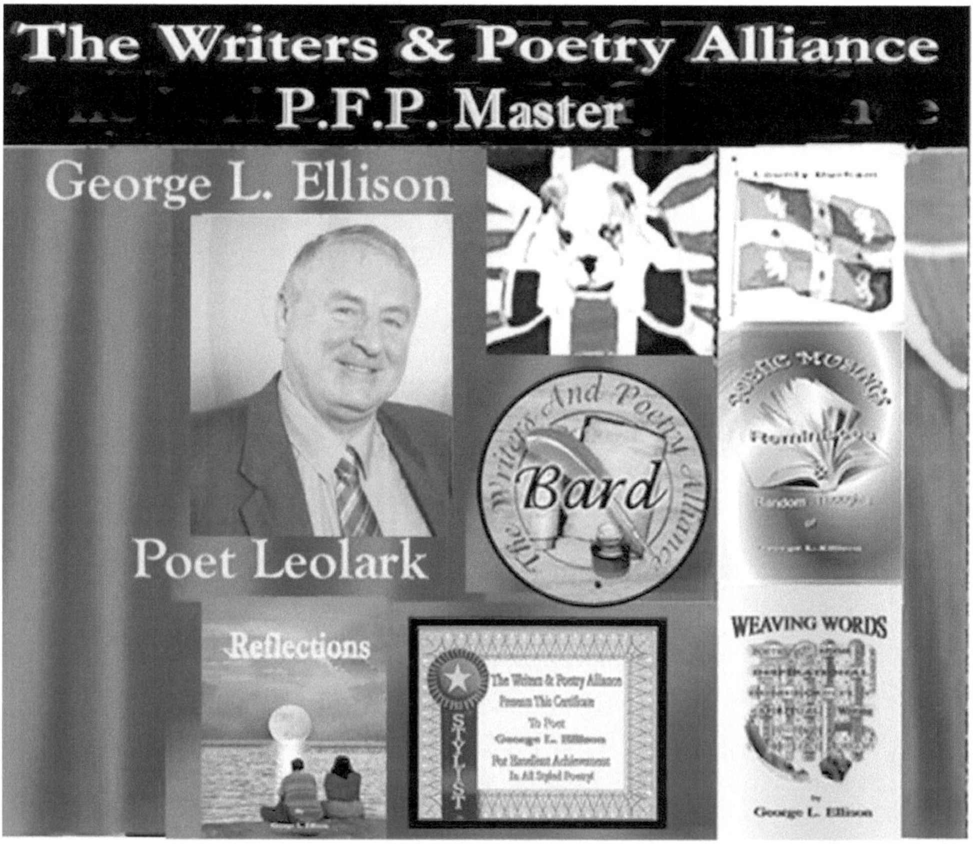

The Writers & Poetry Alliance
P.F.P. Master

George L. Ellison

Poet Leolark

Bard

Reflections

The Writers & Poetry Alliance
Present This Certificate
To Poet
George L. Ellison
For Excellent Achievement
In All Styled Poetry!

STYLIST

WEAVING WORDS

George L. Ellison

http://apfpublisher.com/leolark.html

Christmas Toys

I heard a noise up in the loft,
I climbed up for to see,
It came from all those Christmas toys
That adorns my Christmas tree!
The time is fast approaching,
They sense the mood as well,
When they will be let loose again,
In the living room, for to dwell!

Multi-coloured baubles,
Bright flashing fairy lights,
I can hear them sing and warble-
As they get quite uptight!
"Let us out", I hear them cry,
As the ladder I ascend,
Then descending with said trinkets-
Enough to make the tree bend!

"Hurry up", I hear them cry,
"It's my turn next" they say!
As one by one they make a splash-
Of colour for Christmas day!
They breathe a sigh and grin,
Then they begin to dance and sway,
As they are now awaiting-
Santa and his sleigh!

As they make the room a pleasant place,
On this Christmastide as we dwell,
They fill the home with merriment,
Singing cheery songs and ringing bells!

Pleased to be free once again,
They continue to adorn,
Singing songs of the Christ child,
To pave the way for Christmas morn!
To see the children smile and play,
As presents are given and received,
Presents they are now unwrapped,
What is there here for me?

Christmas day, it comes and goes,
So soon, the year it turns!
The Christmas toys know time is short,
Till to their box, they are returned!
All sealed up for another year,
They go into hibernation,
Till Christmas time comes around again,
When I'll again hear their narration!

Pantomimes

Panto time is here again for the child inside the man

As children of all ages are transported to faerie land

Never land with Peter Pan, Wendy and Captain Hook

The villain, he is behind you if you, at the right time take a look

Oh no he not says he; Oh yes he is we beg

Mother Goose is a favourite with her golden egg

In costume girls are prince's men they are the Dames

Making merry, playing lots of children's games

Every year Panto time, is set aside for family fun

So many love the Pantomimes, picking up on every pun

Trick or Treat

In the darkness of the night
Broomsticks ready to take flight

Ghouls and ghosts they share a joke
As they are prepare to frighten the common folk

Witches and wizards together greet
Where bubbling cauldrons sit on heat

To the cauldron the folk are brought: yet try as they might
As the witches wizards ghouls and ghosts poke
They’ll be given the choice of trick or treat

© George L. Ellison

Horrible Child

I've always been mischievous
It is just the way I am
Since the first day out of pram
I've always been mischievous
I hung teddy on the line
A hanging offence of mine
I've always been mischievous

Getting no better with time
Wriggling worms made sister scream
Torment complete it would seem
Getting no better with time
I would look for more bother
That's the lot of a brother
Getting no better with time

But it's now time to grow up
Be adult in all I do
Still there are moments anew
But it's now time to grow up
When I feel the itch appear
To torment those I hold dear
But it's now time to grow up

© George L. Ellison

April Fools Day

It is April Fool's day
What should I do?
I guess I should play
a little trick on you.
nothing really mean
just having some fun,
A surprise for my queen
something to make her run.
think she's scared of critters
they make her squeal,
give her all kinds jitters
then she'll run in heels,
I got a rubber mouse
hid it where she sits
I will hide in the house
it will give her fits!
It worked like a charm
she can really scream,
She is raising the alarm
time to make the scene.
I picked up the mouse
She didn't think it was funny.
we chased around the house
she hit me with a chocolate bunny.
I tried to say April FOOLS
she call me another name,
she started throwing stools,
but she loves me all the same!

James F. Cunningham

Writers and Poetry Alliance

James F. Cunningham

IN HIS HANDS

Light of the Lord

Reality and Dreams

With Magic in Between

Bard

The Writers And Poetry Alliance

The Writers & Poetry Alliance
Presents This Certificate
To Poet
James F. Cunningham
For Excellent Achievement
In All Styled Poetry!

STYLIST

http://apfpublisher.com/JFC.html

Playful Fairy

The tiny fairy spread her wings
Launched herself into the sky
Heading towards the flowing springs
Because she just loved to fly

Sometimes she would chase a bird
Grabbing at a loose feather
Sometimes she would act absurd
Flying in windy weather

To her it was just a game
That she played all of the time
Until the Queen called her name
She accused her of a crime

Laziness is not allowed
There is too much work to do
Then her tiny head was bowed
She was made to think it through

She knew her work must be done
And she was putting it off
Because it just wasn't fun
The Queen looked at her and coughed

Because she had a silly grin
She promised to make it right
The Queen shook her head again
As she flew out of her sight

Little Cowboy

I dressed up like a cowboy
All the way down to my boots
And my six gun was a toy
That I pretended could shoot

I rode on my hobby horse
Chasing all the bad guys down
And I would catch them of course
Because I could track them down

Sometimes my mother would play
She would always be the judge
And would lock them all away
In between making some fudge

I liked watching cowboy shows
I knew the good guys would win
Sometimes I would start to dose
I would close my eyes and grin

This is me as a child
When kids had to play outside
Some of our games were wild
Until mom called me inside

The Croaking Duo

Dreamed of being a singer,
Who cared what people say.
I was going be a swinger,
Maybe I'll make it one day.

Then a friend joined my band,
We would practice all the time.
We thought we sounded grand,
People said it would be a crime.

We sang in the choir at school,
We thought we must be good.
On that stage felt so cool,
Now we knew we should.

The dynamic duo we would be,
We had to give singing a try.
On stage, so everyone can see,
Mom laughed so hard she cried.

We began to sing then heard a groan,
A person yelled you sound like a toad.
I swear a squishy tomato got thrown,
Then we heard the laughter explode.

We sing now to chase the mice away,
The mailman walked passed our yard.
A few mirrors even cracked one day,
But for one night we actually starred.

The dynamic duo we may never be,
The croaking duo is alive and well.
At least we got our chance to see,
Made one recording we'll never sell.

Playing in the Rain

Raindrops and lollipops;
it's fun to splash around;
at least until it stops,
with puddles on the ground.

Our street was a river;
the rain was coming down.
It was such fun playing,
my heart began to pound.

It was a summer rain;
it didn't last very long.
My Mom said were insane,
but were where we belong.

School is out for summer;
Mom wants us all outside;
sometimes it's a bummer,
she makes us stay inside.

Rainy days are the best,
even though it's muddy;
because our clothes get messed;
Mom's face looks so ruddy.

Because mud's' everywhere,
it's all over the house.
It's even in my hair,
I got myself quite doused.

She puts me in the tub;
scrubs it out of my hair;
she really has to rub,
because it is everywhere.

When I see her smile,
everything is all right.
I know I'm a trial,
as she turns out the light.

My Amazing Life

Oh, it is so amazing
The life I live today
I have no need for anything
Oh Lord, I feel so gay
Life makes me dance and sing, and smile
I don't know why it is
But God did smile on me one day
And filled me full of bliss

I love it in the morning
When I awake from sleep
I love it in the night time
When I rest and sleep, so deep
The sun it shines on me alone
The moon beams just for me
I adore each moment of each day
I am happy just to be.

I have always laughed, and smiled a lot
But it was just skin deep
Until the power smiled at me
And now with joy I weep
I'm happy, happy, happy, happy
I want to scream with joy
My world is filled with only beauty
That nothing could destroy

Peter Duggan

The Writers & Poetry Alliance

Peter Duggan

Bard

Poet Ruby18

http://apfpublisher.com/pedro.html

Fifteen Tiny Swallows

Fifteen tiny swallows
All perched upon a fence
Oh what handsome fellows
But here, let me commence
To speak of all their beauty
These tiny little birds
All black and cream with a reddish throat
Oh how my heart they stirred

A lady walking with her dog
Disturbed these little guys
So from the fence these birds take wing
And head towards the skies
It seems that they are dancing
In the way they fly around
They always seem to fly in circles
And nearly touch the ground.

I walk around these wetlands
And wonder at it all
Everyday it's something else
And it's all so beautiful
Ducks and swallows, parrots too
And the beauty of the lake
I love to walk there most of all
At the coming of the daybreak.

My Dog Bear

Let me tell you about our Bear
He's a great big, clumsy beast
He's got to be one hundred pound
That's at the very least

Now he's a crazy Rottweiler
He's supposed to be pretty mean
Yet really he's a great big softie
Aggression I've never seen

Our Bear is such a blessed wimp
One day while we were out
He nearly had me fly above him
As he dragged me all about

There was some thunder in the sky
That sure did frighten him
Next think he's got me almost flying
As I'm hanging on like grim

He stopped at last, I was a mess
All bruised and bleeding some
And me I was so very angry
That he had been so dumb

He looked at me with big sad eyes
Then all that I could do
Was give him a stroke, and a gentle pat
But I'm a softie too.

© Peter Duggan

My Mo In law

My Mo in law, she's ninety five
And wow, she's looking bright
I see her in that old folk's home
She looks a real delight
Though she can't get around much now
She still delights in life
With a smile to all who pass on by
She seems so free from strife

She came out here at twenty nine
To our good sunny land
She worked so hard when she came here
And she made no demands
Milking cows there on the farm
Bringing up three kids
And she got on without a moan
In everything she did.

She helped her husband build two homes
She worked and worked all day
She done each thing she had to do
In a sweet and gentle way
On thinking about my Mo in law
I'd have to tell you this
Old Rosie she's a mighty bird
You know, she really is.

A Happy Home

It's a happy home round here
With lots of harmony
Cause happy is the way we are
Don't need no misery
I wake up with each new morn
And write my Vee a poem
I think she really likes this too
It seems, sometimes she's glowing.

Then we have our Daughter Li
And my cheeky grand-son Jake
They get me laughing all the time
Old Jake he's wide awake
He twists his mum into a pretzel
As they bicker constantly
It's just a happy game they play
That's plain enough to see

And me who once was grumpy

I'm jolly now, and sweet

And when I walk into a room

Most everyone I meet

Will meet me with a happy smile

I no longer am a threat

So now I go along in life

With nothing to regret

Kitchen Comedy Hour

Seems that Mr Bengay is here to stay.
Hank does use before work each new day.
The cats do enjoy smell.
You just can always tell.
They tag each other as in relay.

They get frisky like they used to be.
Happily playing; I like to see.
They wrestle each other.
They cherish their Mother.
They then both play hide and seek with me.

Golly Bengay smell did make me sneeze.
My sinus did feel a little ease.
The cats seemed to get high.
Josh jumped up in the sky
Magic then joined in to give a tease.

Next Magic tried to lick Hank's bad knee.
This was something so funny to see.
We then let him go out.
The others played about.
Hope it does fix the way it should be.

Christina R Jussaume

Alliance Style Tutor

AKA
Poet
Crj147

Bard

Christina R. Jussaume
Style Tutor Manager

The Writers & Poetry Alliance
Presents This Certificate
Style Tutor
Christina R Jussaume
For Excellent Achievement
In All Styled Poetry!

STYLIST

http://apfpublisher.com/Tina.html

• The Royal Chipmunk's Request

• The royal chipmunk made Queen a request
He knew the royal Queen would do her best
He had a real near escape with his life
The episode did give Queen's maid some strife

He entered the stump feeder for a meal
The stray cat did put him through an ordeal
It was near empty and he went in
The cat waited near entrance so he'd win

• The Queen's maid had gone in to fill bin
She was startled as chipmunk was within
He squealed in fright and she screamed back at him
She chased away cat as things looked real dim

She waited a while and then went back out
Again the scared chipmunk did start to shout!
Her heart and blood pressure had gone sky high!
It was then that she turned to God to pray

She then left garden and started to pray
She returned and scooted chipmunk away
She was then able to fill the feeder
Chipmunk returns as family leader

A request was made for chipmunk to Queen
Could they befriend cat, so he would not be mean?

Breakdancing Squirrel

Hank was Breakdancing Squirrel,
In forest taught others by referral
Lined up by his large Oak tree,
They gathered as they bended knee
Music played by Songbird chorus,
Clapping hands led by wife Doris
Forest laughter heard by all,
Comradery here surely did enthrall!

Chloe's Story

I am a pretty girl kitty
I was a shelter cat in past
I have a friend called Tinkerbelle
She and I cuddle and feels swell
She goes outside not wearing bell
Home here I hope to last

I am well fed and brushed each day
Routine starts with Fancy Feast food
Sit on back of couch looking out
Glad watching hummingbird about
Days are filled with love never doubt
I'm always in good mood

Before had two litters on own
I was trapped; then they tipped my ear
My days are filled with greatest love
I even watch mourning dove
God I thank you from up above
My family is dear!

- © Christina R Jussaume

Knock, Knock

What's making that knocking sound below?
I then walk down to my cellar slow
Rinse cycle wash now on
I am tired and yawn
It was a wild turkey that I know!

On window he continues to knock
He is smaller not from the known flock
He just does peck, peck, peck!
I now do feel a wreck
Afraid of window breaking I squawk!

I go outside to chase him away
I feed but hope this one doesn't stay
Went out few times to chase
Thought was play and a race
He looks like young one that wants to play!

Cat Box Dilemma

Cat boxes need to be cleaned each day
Having four cats; that is what they say
It can be easy too,
If you keep scoop in view
Throwing scoop out is not correct way!

Felt stupid when I had to tell cat
Garbage went out; scoop did too; that's fact!
Had to travel to store,
To do the dirty chore
It was not pristine; imagine that!

They waited in anticipation
When I came home; they felt elation!
Josh waited until clean
Then it was smelly scene!
Have extra scoop for situation

Cashier thought I was really quite nuts
I explained was to help keep clean butts
She smiled as she rang up
I drank water from cup
Got to run now; they just might erupt!

The Barnyard Animals

Cock- a- Doodle Doo the rooster wakes you
He struts across the yard; that is so true
Molly moves Mooing as moves to milking station,
She is happy and filled with elation!

Meowing Mouser Meagan stops for milk,
The food she eats makes her fur soft like silk
Chirping Cardinal sings as she does warn,
Their song is such a pleasure early dawn!

Baa-Baa Bleats the sheep as hears commotion,
She does reply with love and devotion
Cocky Cackling hens begin barnyard dance,
Rocky Raccoon is annoyed and does prance!

Barnyard noise awakes farmer that's inside,
Rocky Raccoon must scatter now, lose pride
Bow-wow Barks Bernard as hens do scatter,
He's around now so it will not matter!

The Elves and The Editor

Deadline day is drawing nigh
The editor slumps and wipes an eye.
Fifty poems to review and rank one by one.
No sleep, gonna be rough before she's done.

An Elf bouncing about the room with mirth
Looking for a victim of sorts to unearth.
He sees this lovely lass with drooping lids.
Decides to bring along all his kids.

They climbed all over her chair and hair
Laughing and bouncing in the air.
Kissing her cheek and tickling her chin.
Finally getting a nice little grin.

Her spirits rise and she knows what to do.
She tosses the poems, they scattered and blew.
Catching two in the air she let the others face doom.
She joins the elves and dances around the room.

Robert Hewett Sr

The Writers & Poetry Alliance

Poet Cottonwood

Robert Hewett Sr.

aka "Bob"

Laureate

http://apfpublisher.com/Cotton.html

Pot Hole Delight

I'm a little pothole hidden from the light.
Every time a tire hits me it is a delight.
The more that hit me the bigger I get,
Waiting for a low slung hot rider, you bet.

Here comes an eighteen wheeler crusin' past
Nine big tires making me bigger real fast.
Such a loud bang, bounce and shudder,
Makes me so happy I feel like butter.

Little old ladies, and some younger ones too,
Never think to swerve, the right thing to do.
No real joy there, I just grin and blend in.
Old guys swear at me and the city repairmen.

The greatest thrill that I ever get on any given day
Is when a road hog without mufflers comes my way.
Low slung and reclining way back,
He can never see a pothole and that's a fact.

All is well, and happy I am indeed
Causing breakdowns and discomfort is my need.
Oh no, they finally get here in that redhot truck
To cover me over with tar and muck.

I am asleep now invisible to all
I await the rain and sun this summer or fall.
I will be back, you can bet on that.
So, say goodnight and tip your hat.

The Big Christmas Sale

It was in the papers and told on all the news
Come to the Mall at five a. m. and you could choose
Great gifts free, if you are one of the first fifty.
Good ones like computers and Xboxes so nifty.

I had a plan that, to me, was foolproof and safe too.
I would wait all night and be the first one through.
I didn't make number one, but I was third in line,
Sitting on my stool and freezing all the time.

The big doors flew wide open right on schedule
The crowd rushed the doors like stampeding cattle.
I jumped up, lost my footing, and fell to the ground,
Nobody noticed or even bothered to go around.

I lay there, covered my head, and prayed out loud
Lord, send the high heel shoes to the mall downtown.
The rush was soon over and I managed to rise,
Clothes torn, but all in one piece much to my surprise.

I entered the store to get my low cost gifts,
I held out the paper and gave my belt a lift.
The clerk just looked, laughed and picked up a curler.
Try again next year, but you need to be earlier.

How to Catch a Skunk

We read it in print, my brother and me,
Skunks make wonderful pets for all to see.
The one in the magazine was descented.
I seriously doubt the skunk had consented.
It seemed like a fun summer adventure,
We knew just how we would catch this creature.
A skunk has two ways to escape its lair
We had a plan to capture him right there.
My brother was twelve and I was just eight,
We planned to go there right after we ate.
A burlap sack and dog Tip, was our plan
To catch this skunk quickly by our own hand.
Our really great plan was fully thought out.
All angles explored and bandied about.
Tip would bark and dig one end of the lair
We would wait at the other hole with care.

The plan was so simple, it could not fail
My job was to just grab hold of its tail,
Hold it down so that he wouldn't spray
As my brother quickly stuffed him away.
Our perfect plan was now working very good.
Tip was barking and digging, we knew he would.
The pitter patter of the skunk's fast feet,
Told us that our plan was nearly complete.

His Tail came out, then his hopping hind feet.
I pulled his furry tail down, it felt neat.
Everything was going just as we planned
Until he turned, trying to bite my hand.
I let go and ran fast to Dad in the field
Skunk sprayed my brother's face full while he kneeled.
My brother still stuffed the skunk in the sack
Shook his head and brought the skunk and sack back.

My Brother and the Bee Tree

My brother was home on Army leave.
Every girls' nightly dream he did believe.
He strolled around our farm without a shirt
To show his muscles and maybe to flirt.
Dad called out "let's go rob a honey tree".
The idea certainly sounded good to me.
We gathered our saw, axe and smoke bellows
And headed to the woods feeling mellow.

We went to the pond where the bees came alone,
And used line of sight to follow them home.
My dad, Haskell, Buster and me.
Plus Snowball, Buster's dog at his knee.

Buster did not have on his shirt,
So he stood back so he wouldn't get hurt.
The honey was in an old hollow tree,
Dad and I sawed it down one two three.
The tree hit the ground and the bees were swarming,
Buzzing loudly their hysterical warning.
Dad used the smoker to quiet them down
then made a hole for the honey we found.

Snowball came up to take a sniff and a look
The bees covered her like a cover on a book.
Straight to Buster, his howling dog ran,
Wanting protection from the angry bee clan.

Buster had other thoughts on his mind,
He was racing through the woods making time,
Snowball and the bees kept up just fine.
"Go away Snowball, Go away", he cried.
I found my brother out in the pond
Snowball beside him not having fun.
Under water they had found a place
Safe from the bees still in the chase.

El Penon

Saturday morning off we run
To the football ground El Penon
In Puerto De La Cruz to see
Young lads playing so happily

Young lads learn to play happily
With family in support totally
To see home team or visitor
Kicking ball in goal to score

At El Penon we love to see
Young boys improve and agree
Football's great with time to spare
Using up energy with great flair

To the football ground El Penon
Boys give all they've got till game's done
If Puerto loses then we don't care
While boys enjoy the game they share

Saturday morning off we run
To hear whistle goes off like a gun
When games done then we say
"It's great to see the young boys play"

Patricia Ann Farnsworth-Simpson

http://apfpublisher.com/Pat.html

Santa “Where's My Teddy”

Santa Claus brought brother Wilf a Teddy bear
Our David got one too which I didn’t think fair
He brought me the latest doll with blinking eyes
To another girl it would be a good surprise

But I couldn’t cuddle a doll that was made of pot
Or the lovely pram it sat in that it had got
Our Wilf and David both loved their Teddy's so
They carry and hug them wherever they'd go

They’d bounce Teddy on knee laughing at me
Because they knew that I was so jealous you see
They’d say “Why don’t you go get your doll to play
Instead of sitting there watching us all day”

I’d cry “Why hasn’t He brought me a Teddy too
One I could cuddle and bounce on my knees like you”
“Because you are a girl and its dolls that you get
So clear off and play with yours and never forget

That Teddy’s belong to boys in this house
Not to you little girl so stop this grouse”
I did but behind their backs I’d grab their Teddy
To cuddle real tight close to me!

My Very First Dip

Time was when of my own accord
To stop myself from being bored
I'd shoot off with my surfboard
To sail on the river I adored.

Then if I got bored on a whim
I would dive in the river for a swim
In the water that I once did skim
On my surfboard looking prim

Truly being in and near water I love
Though my very first dip came with a shove
From my brother who I suppose sort of
Wanted some peace and me rid of

Though I guess just for ten minutes or so
But it truly didn't work you know
Because I enjoyed it and with face aglow
I shouted "Come on in and have a go"

He did but only to get me out
"Then keep your mouth shut" he did shout
"Don't tell our Dad for without a doubt
If I get a slap, then you'll get a clout"

BBQ is Great

I love to go for BBQ
Round many, many bends
Up through woods with my friends
Where much comradeship blends

Families there altogether
Enjoy each other so
Conversation does flow
With all age groups on show

Grand parents play with the young ones
On nibbles they're sucking
Whilst Mothers not looking
And Dad does the cooking

When all have eaten feeling great
Enjoying glass of wine
Toasting each other fine
BBQ is great time

© Patricia Ann Farnsworth-Simpson

Playing Games

I love to play card games, dominoes too...
Either solo or with a partner grand
Who always somehow seems to know
what is in my hand
On many an afternoon we play
love it I surely do
A real good session
After a swim in the sea so blue

It's in bar Vino Tinto we play
Listening to a much-loved song
The landlord plays in the back ground
That if winning I hum along
With happiness in this lovely bar
If I'm winner then dance I do
But win or not I enjoy playing
At cards and dominoes too

© Patricia Ann Farnsworth-Simpson

Angels of the Deep

A school of Water Angels swim in the sea
Willing to help all in trouble they see
They're sleek and smooth and they can fly
With one leap out the ocean into the sky!

They're Angels because they bring delight
To make sick children's eyes sparkling bright
They give joy to all as they laugh and play
Making everyone glad they're in our world today!

They bring healing to all in their own special way
By putting joy in the heart that will ever stay
If in trouble in the ocean they're known to be
A willing helper to save you from the sea!

If you touch them you'll find they feel like you
Not slimy like a fish like you'd think they do
No! Their flesh is warm just like yours and mine
Through love within them that is divine

Yes! They are truly Angels of the deep
Angels that you'll never see fall asleep
But always swimming freely in the ocean wide
Filling you with a joy you cannot hide

These Angels are called Dolphins by man
Though they have no wings that we see span
They have the heart that's needed for them to be
An Angel from Heaven living in the sea!

Our Muse to Move Book

http://www.lulu.com/shop/poets-world-wide/muse-to-move/paperback/product-23160191.html

Some of Our Fund Raising Books

A Passionately Fair Publisher
Always Here To Help You Achieve Your Literary Dreams
The Writers And Poetry Alliance
Bard
Fiction
Novels
Stories
Pat Simpson
Poetry
Rhymes
Fables
Contact E Mail: apfpublisher@gmail.com

www.ingramcontent.com/pod-product-compliance
Ingram Content Group UK Ltd.
Pitfield, Milton Keynes, MK11 3LW, UK
UKHW041937190726
13854UKWH00004B/1650

9 781387 975358